HAL LEONARD
BASS
TAB METHOD
SONGBOOK

ISBN 978-1-4803-4587-4

HAL•LEONARD®
CORPORATION
7777 W. BLUEMOUND RD. P.O. BOX 13819 MILWAUKEE, WI 53213

Visit Hal Leonard Online at
www.halleonard.com

TABLE OF CONTENTS

Beverly Hills

Words and Music by Rivers Cuomo

Key of F

Intro
Moderately slow

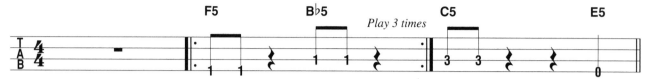

Verse

1. Where I come from isn't all that great. My automobile is a piece of
2. Look at all those movie stars, they're all so beautiful and clean.

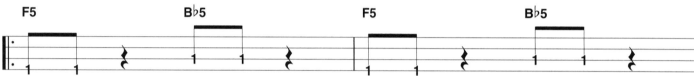

crap. My fashion sense is a little whack and my friends are just as screwy as
When the housemaids scrub the floors they get the spaces in between.

me. I didn't go to boarding schools, preppy girls never looked at
I wanna live a life like that, I wanna be just like a king.
(3.) I'm just a no - class beat - down fool and I will always be that

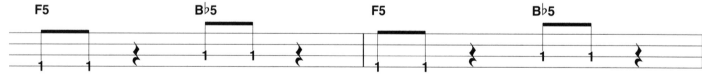

me. Why should they? I ain't no - body, got nothin' in my pocket.
Take my picture by the pool 'cause I'm the next big thing.
way. I might as well enjoy my life and watch the stars play.

Chorus

Beverly Hills, that's where I want to be. Living in Beverly Hills.

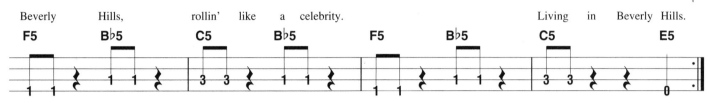

3rd time, To Coda ⊕

Beverly Hills, rollin' like a celebrity. Living in Beverly Hills.

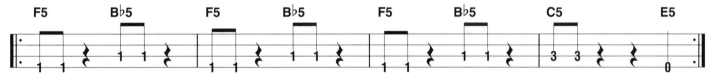

Guitar Solo

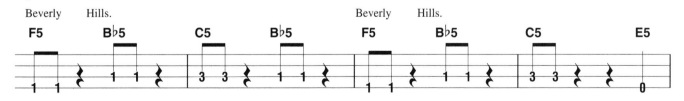

D.S. al Coda

Interlude

Spoken: The truth is, I don't stand a chance. It's something you're born into and I just don't belong. 3. No, I don't,

⊕ Coda

Beverly Hills.   Beverly Hills.

Beverly Hills.   Beverly Hills.   Living in Beverly Hills.

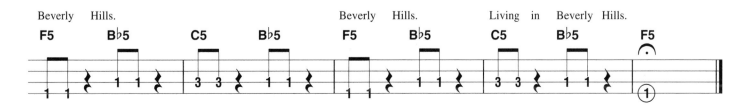

Born Under a Bad Sign

Words and Music by Booker T. Jones and William Bell

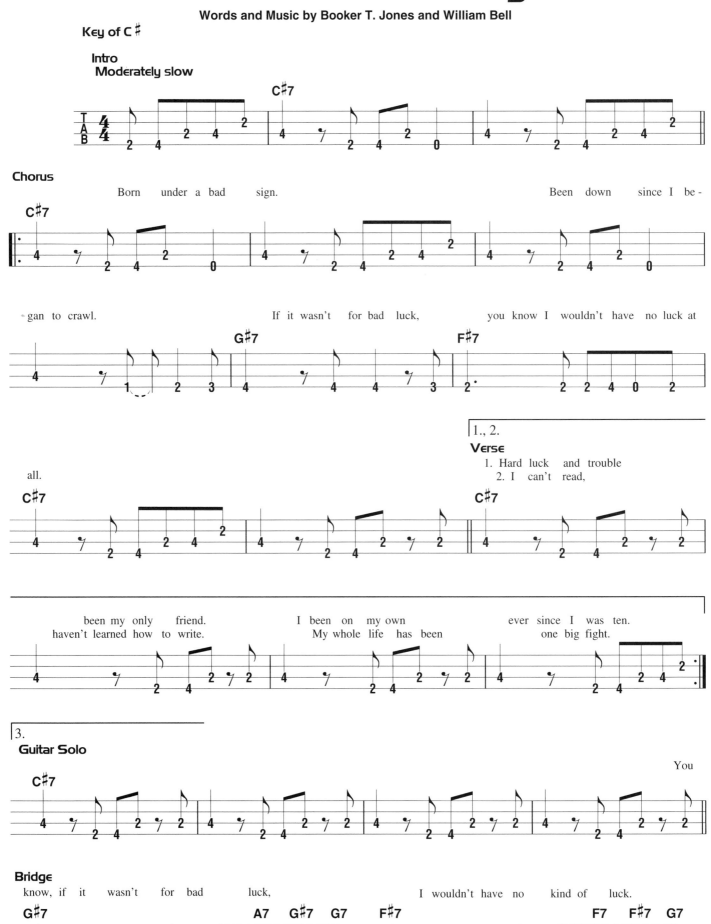

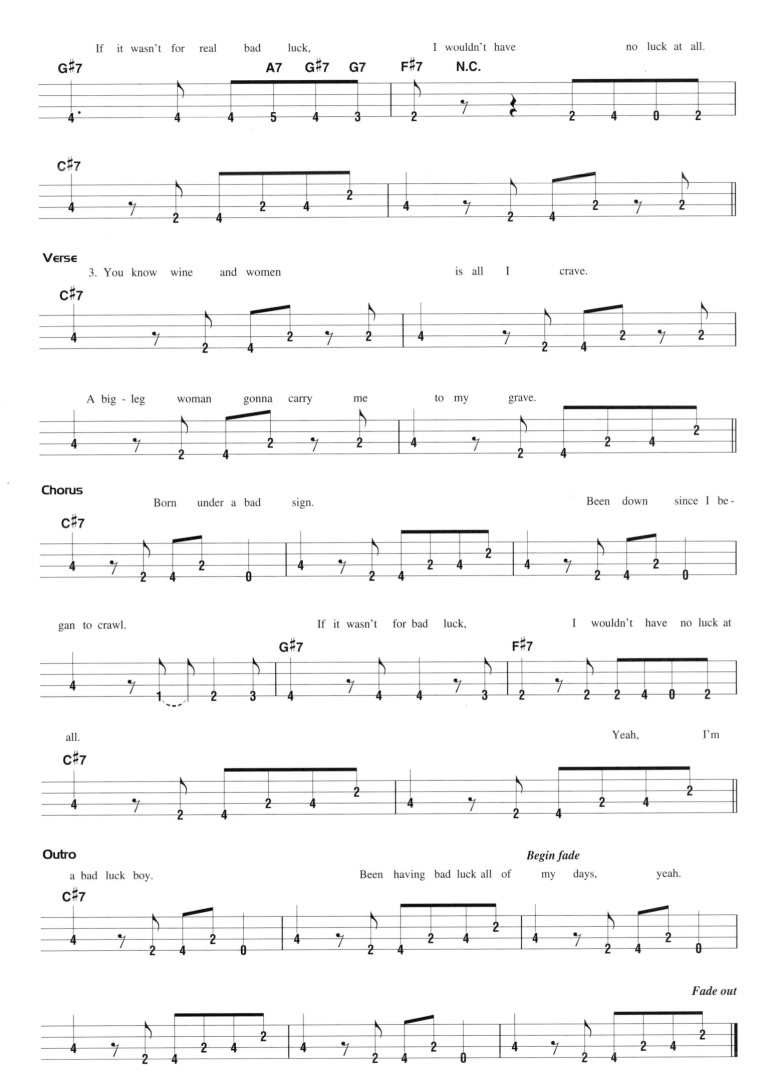

Brown Eyed Girl

Words and Music by Van Morrison

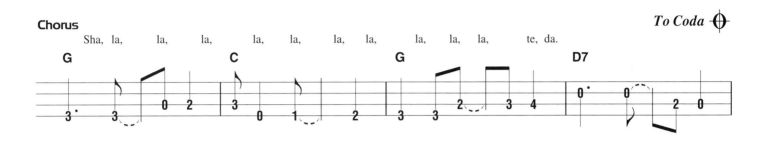

Chorus

To Coda ⊕

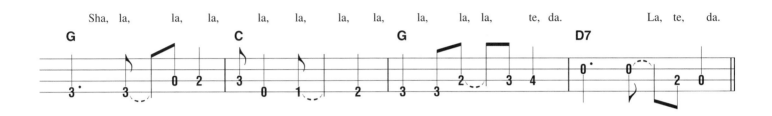

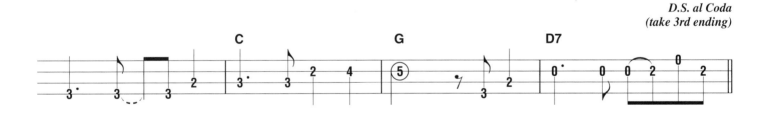

D.S. al Coda
(take 3rd ending)

⊕ **Coda**

Repeat & fade

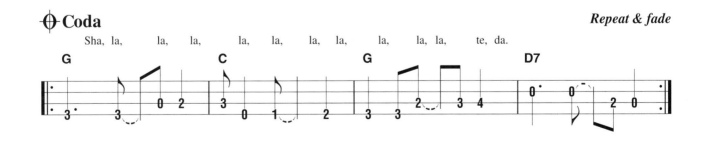

Additional Lyrics

2. Now whatever happened to Tuesday and so slow,
   Going down the old mine with a transistor radio?
   Standing in the sunlight laughing, hiding behind a rainbow's wall.
   Slipping and a sliding all along the waterfall with you,
   My brown eyed girl.

3. So hard to find my way now that I'm all on my own.
   I saw you just the other day; my, how you have grown.
   Cast my mem'ry back there, lord.
   Sometimes I'm overcome thinkin' about it.
   Making love in the green grass
   Behind the stadium with you, my brown eyed girl.

Hey Joe

Words and Music by Billy Roberts

Key of E

Intro
Moderately fast

N.C.

(Guitar)

Verse

1. Hey, Joe, where you goin' with that
2. Hey, Joe, I heard you shot your

gun in your hand?
woman down, shot her down, now.

Hey, Joe, I said, where you goin' with that
Hey, Joe, I heard you shot your

gun in your hand?
lady down, you shot her down in the ground.

I'm goin' down to shoot my old lady, you know I caught her messin' 'round with an -
Yes, I did, I shot her you know I caught her messin' 'round,

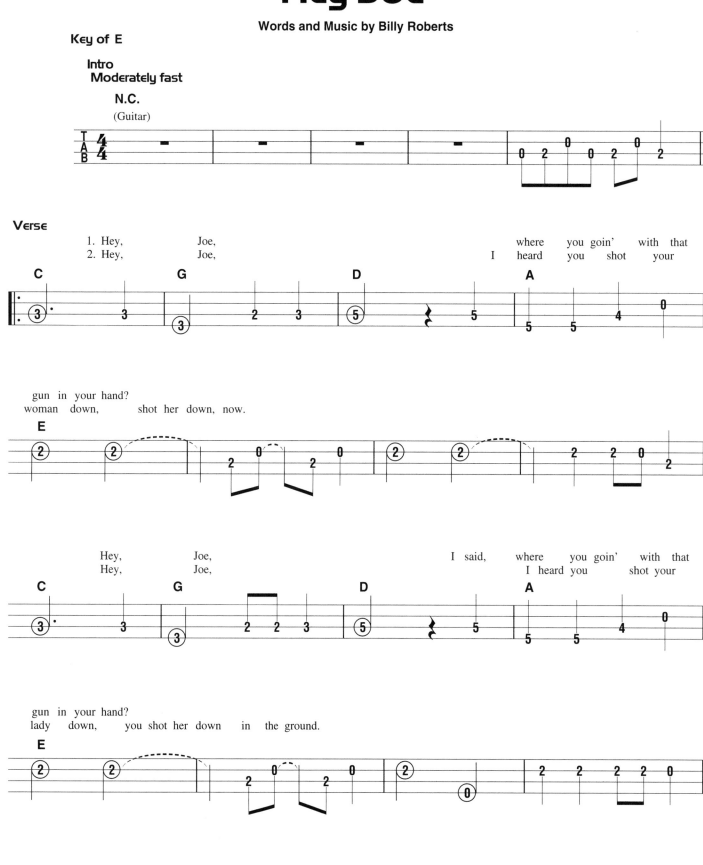

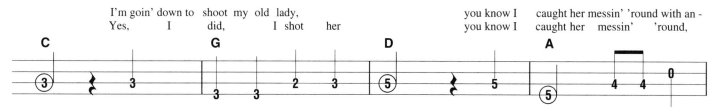

another man.
messin' around   town.

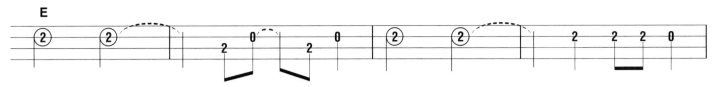

I'm goin' down to shoot   my   old   lady,   you know I   caught   her messin' 'round with an -
Yes,   I   did,   I   shot   her.   You know I   caught   my old lady messin' 'round,

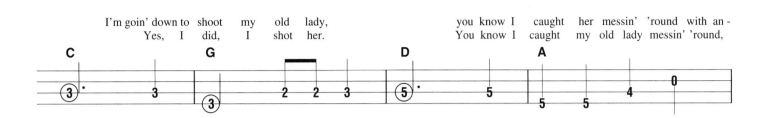

other man.   And   that   ain't   too cool.
town.   And   I   gave   her the   gun.   I shot   her!

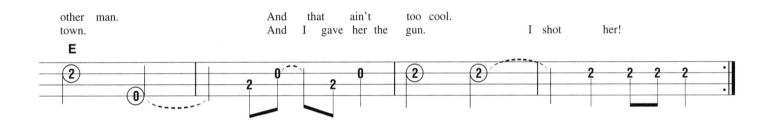

Guitar Solo

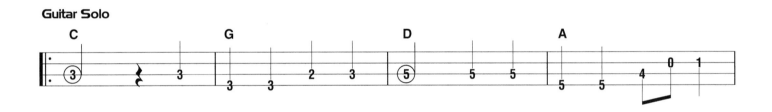

Outro

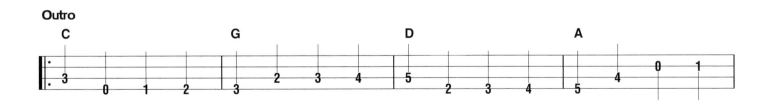

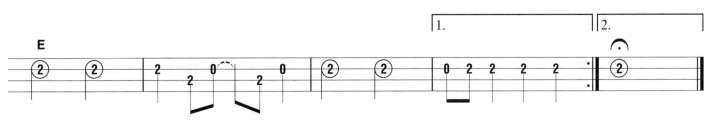

I Won't Back Down

Words and Music by Tom Petty and Jeff Lynne

Key of G

Intro
Moderately

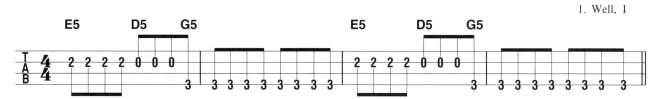

1. Well, I

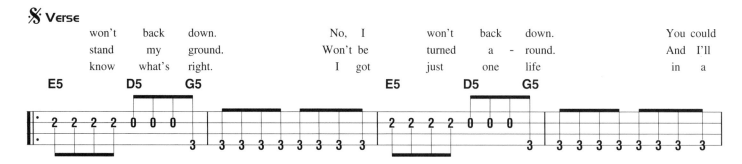

𝄋 Verse

won't   back   down.   No, I   won't   back   down.   You could
stand   my   ground.   Won't be   turned   a - round.   And I'll
know   what's   right.   I   got   just   one   life   in a

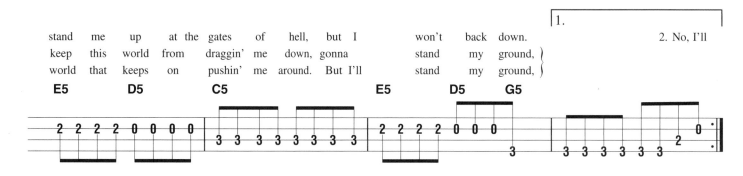

stand   me   up   at the   gates   of   hell,   but I   won't   back   down.
keep   this   world   from   draggin'   me   down,   gonna   stand   my   ground,
world   that   keeps   on   pushin'   me   around.   But I'll   stand   my   ground,

1.   2. No, I'll

2.

and   I   won't   back   down.   (I won't back down.)

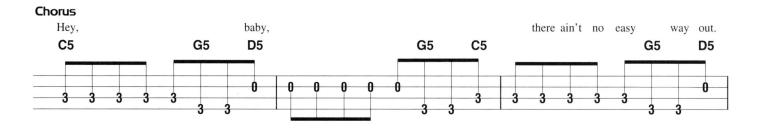

Chorus

Hey,   baby,   there ain't   no   easy   way   out.

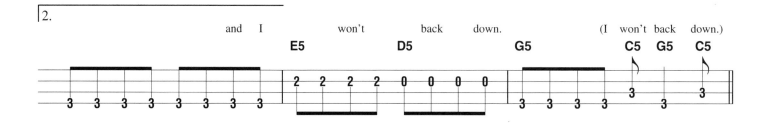

(I won't back   down.) Hey,   I   will

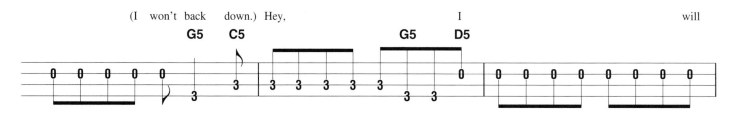

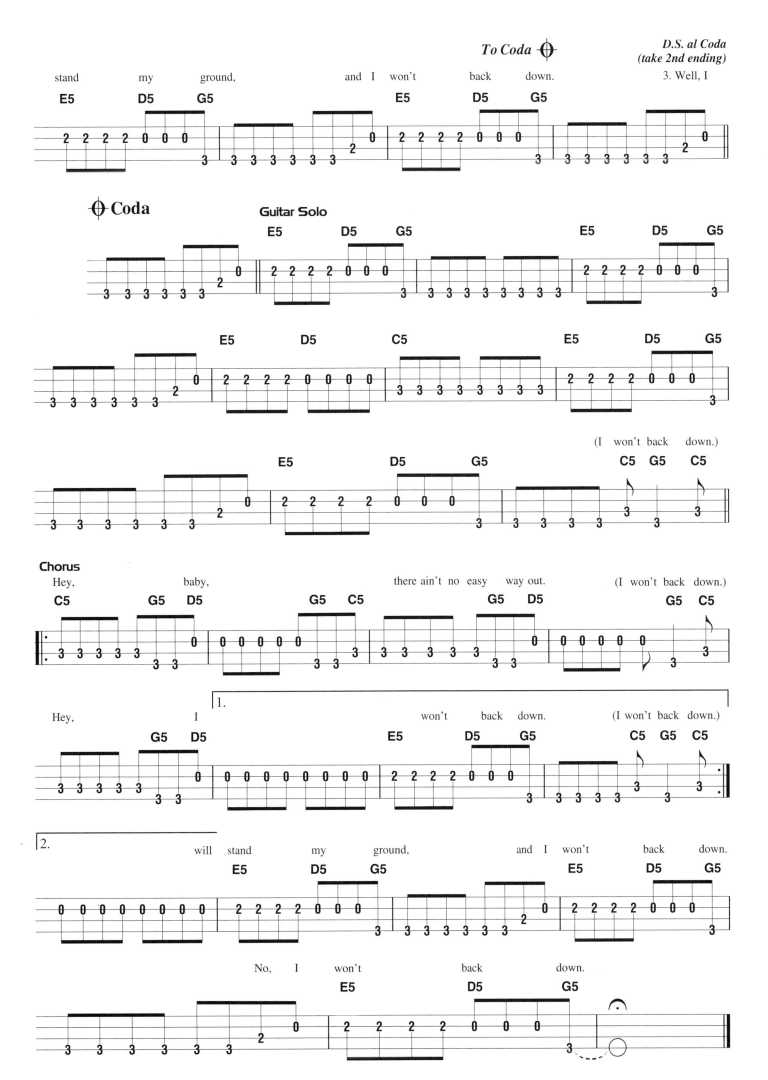

Smoke on the Water

Words and Music by Ritchie Blackmore, Ian Gillan, Roger Glover, Jon Lord and Ian Paice

Key of Gm

Intro
Moderately

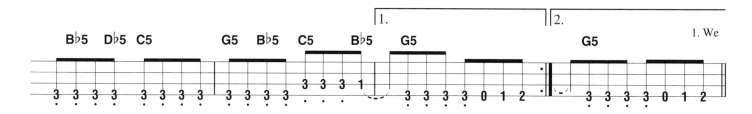

Verse

all came out to Mon - treaux   on the Lake Geneva   shore - line

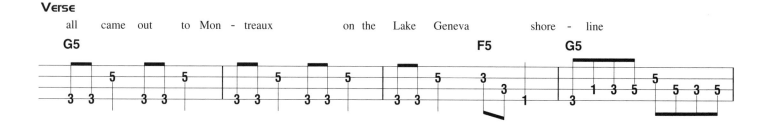

to make records   with the mobile,   we didn't have much time.

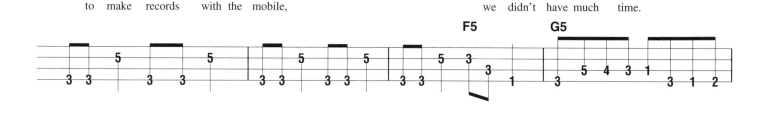

But Frank Zappa   and the Mothers   were at the best place   around.

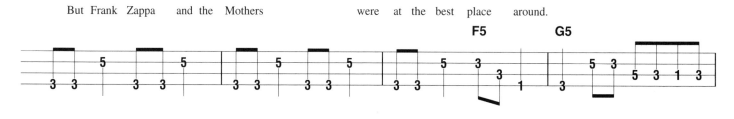

But some stupid   with a flare gun   burned the place   to the   ground.

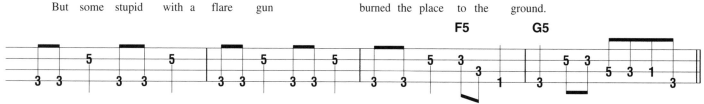

Chorus

Smoke   on the water,   a fire   in the sky.

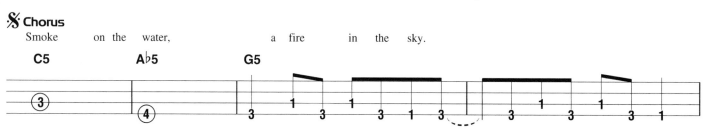

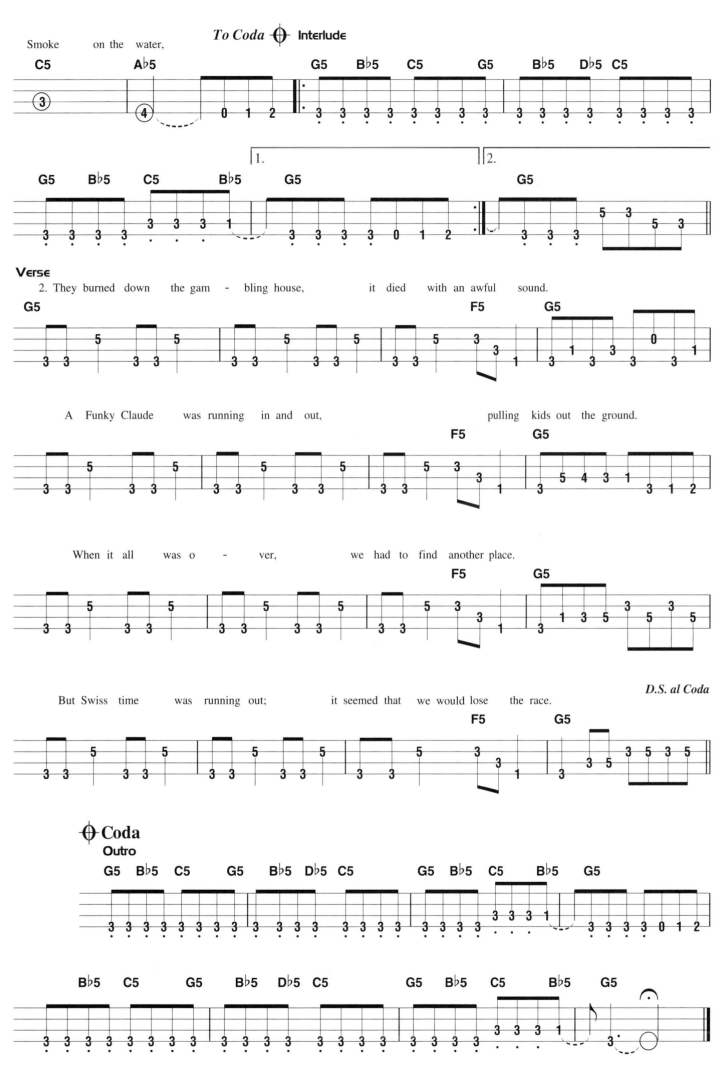

Stir It Up

Words and Music by Bob Marley

Key of A

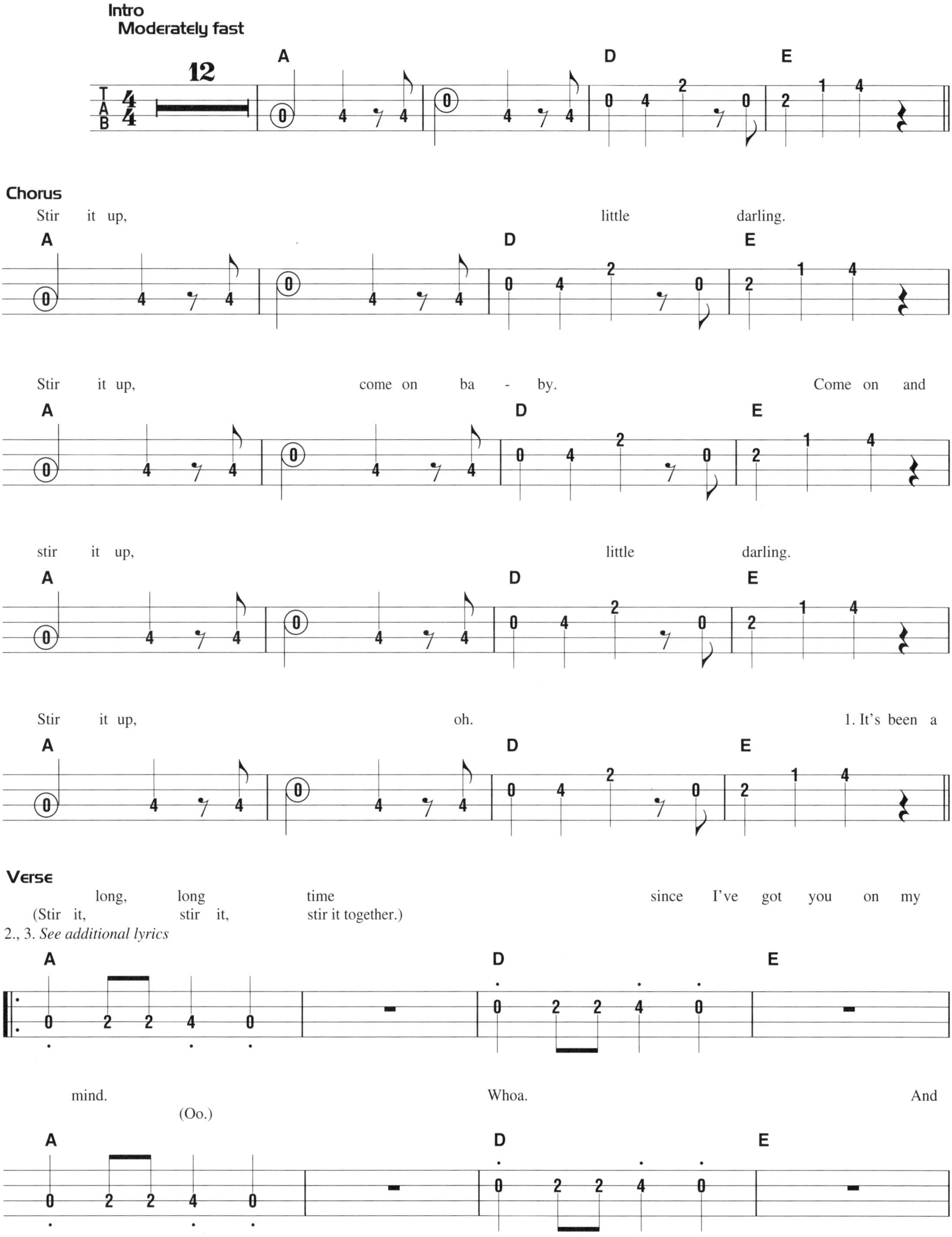

Intro
Moderately fast
12
A D E
Chorus
Stir it up, little darling.
A D E
Stir it up, come on ba - by. Come on and
A D E
stir it up, little darling.
A D E
Stir it up, oh. 1. It's been a
A D E
Verse
long, long time since I've got you on my
(Stir it, stir it, stir it together.)
2., 3. See additional lyrics
A D E
mind. Whoa. And
(Oo.)
A D E

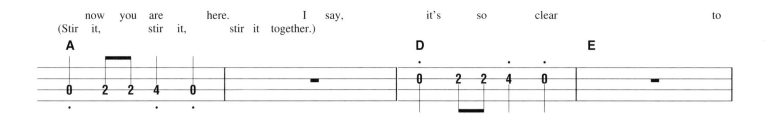

now you are here. I say, it's so clear to
(Stir it, stir it, stir it together.)

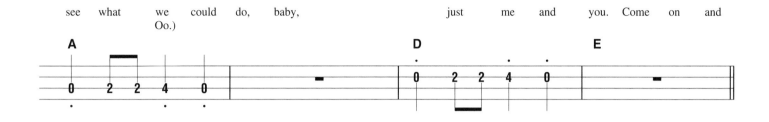

see what we could do, baby, just me and you. Come on and
Oo.)

Chorus

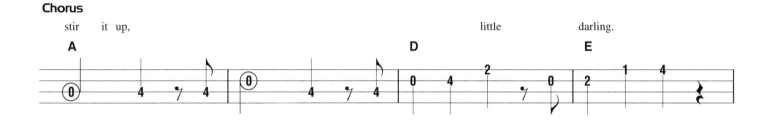

stir it up, little darling.

Stir it up, come on ba - by. Come on and

stir it up, little darling.

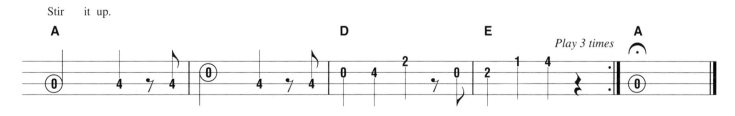

Stir it up.

Play 3 times

Additional Lyrics

2. I'll push the wood, and I'll blaze your fire.
   Then I satisfy your heart's desires.
   Said I stir it, yeah, every minute.
   All you've got to do, baby, is keep it in it and stir it up.

3. And then quench me when I'm thirsty.
   Come on, cool me down, baby, when I'm hot.
   Your recipe, darling, is so tasty.
   And you sure can stir your pot. So, stir it up.

Use Somebody

Words and Music by Caleb Followill, Nathan Followill, Jared Followill and Matthew Followill

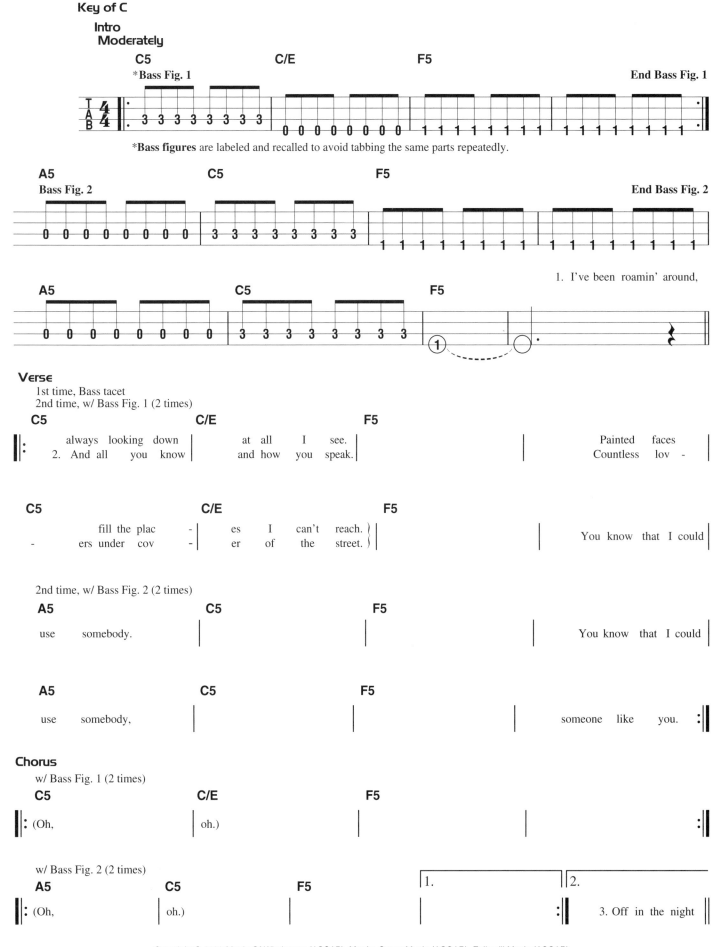

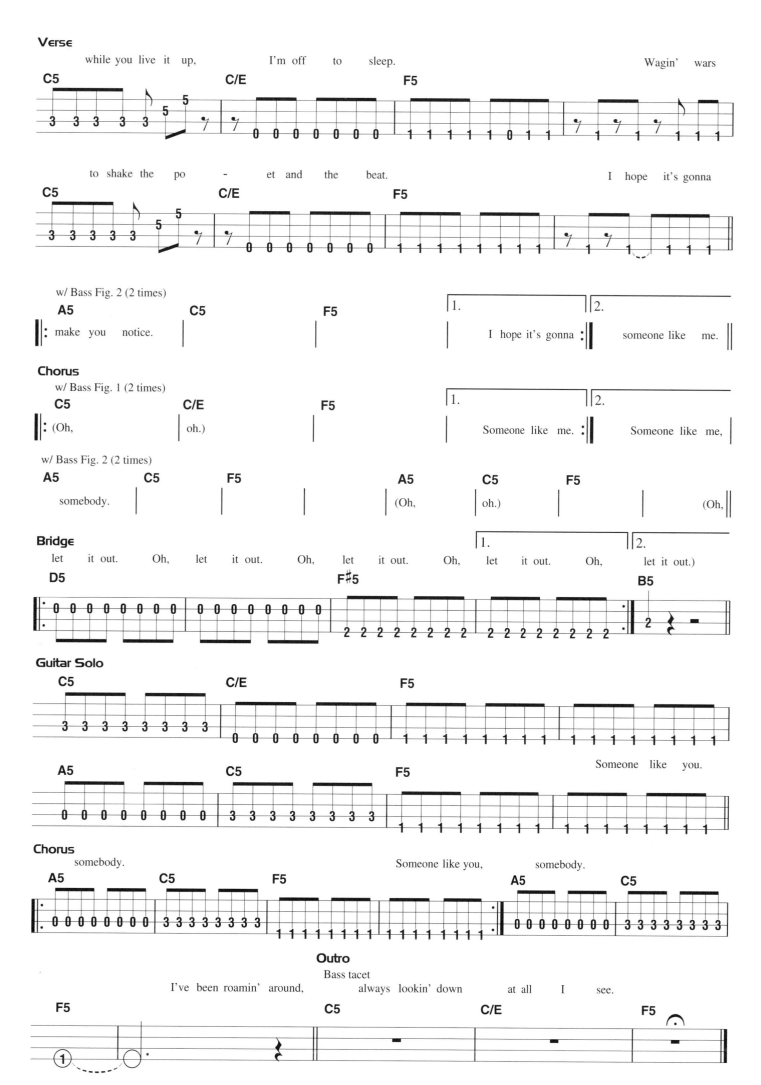

You Are the Sunshine of My Life

Words and Music by Stevie Wonder

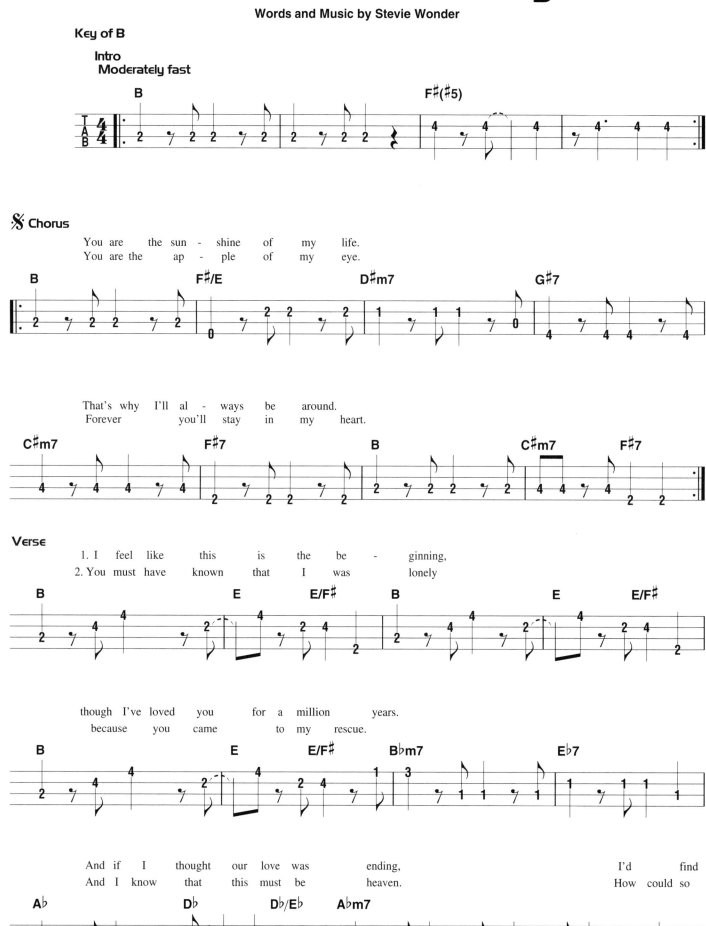

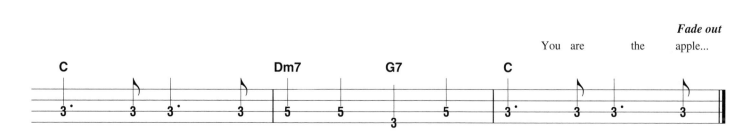

To Coda
D.S. al Coda
(take repeat)
myself drown - ing in my own tears. Whoa, whoa.
much love be inside of
C♯7
F♯sus4
Coda
Key of C
Chorus
you? Whoa, whoa. You are the sun - shine of my
You are the ap - ple of my
F♯7sus4
Gsus4
C
G/F
life, yeah. That's why I'll al - ways stay a -
eye. Forever you stay in the heart.
Em7
A7
Dm7
G7
Begin fade
round. You are the sun - shine of my
C
Dm7
G7
C
G/F
life, baby. That's why I'll al - ways stay around.
Em7
A7
Dm7
F/G
Fade out
You are the apple...
C
Dm7
G7
C

Crazy Train

Words and Music by Ozzy Osbourne, Randy Rhoads and Bob Daisley

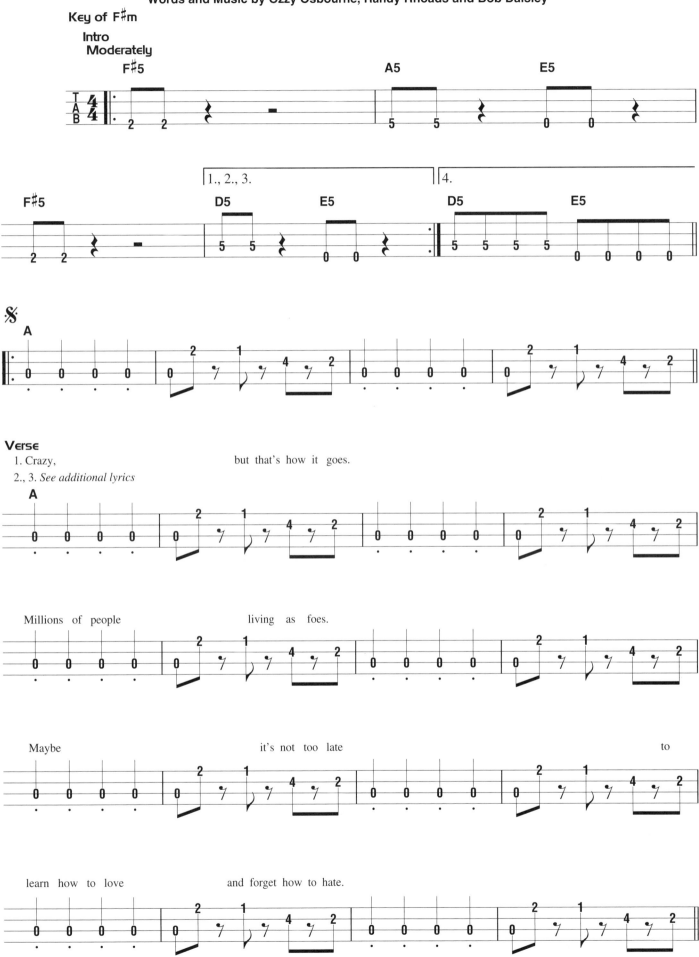

Chorus

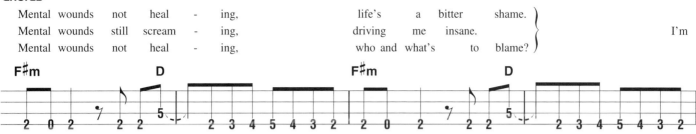

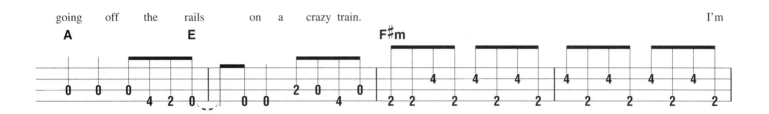

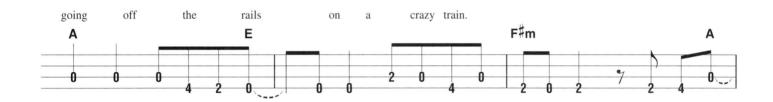

To Coda ⊕

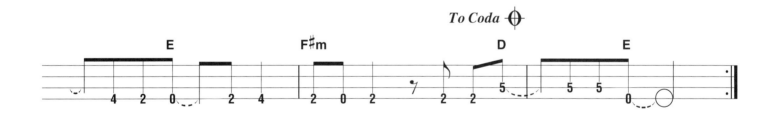

Bridge

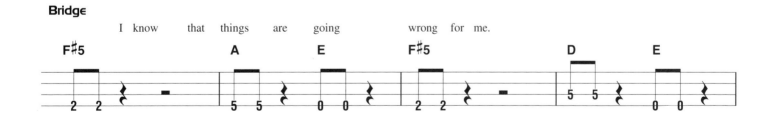

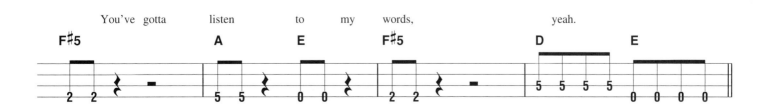

Guitar Solo

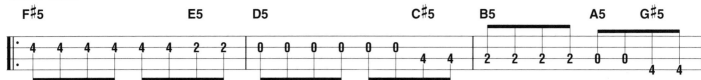

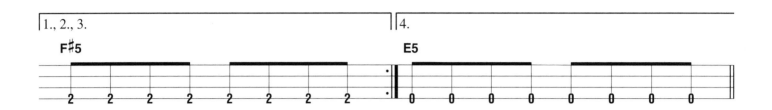

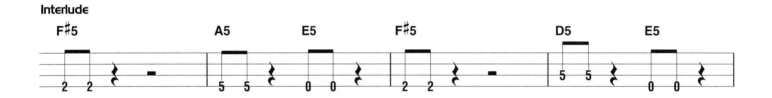

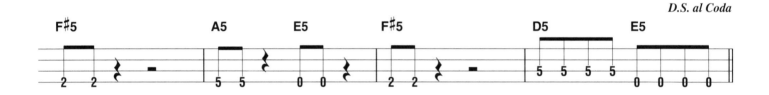

D.S. al Coda

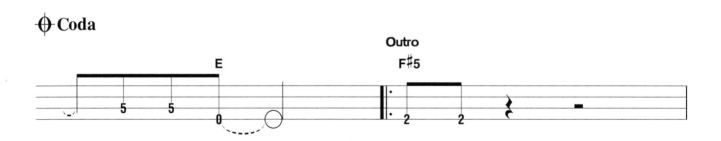

Coda

Outro

Repeat and fade

Additional Lyrics

2. I've listened to preachers, I've listened to fools.
   I've watched all the dropouts who make their own rules.
   One person conditioned to rule and control.
   The media sells it and you live the role.

3. Heirs of the cold war, that's what we've become.
   Inheriting troubles, I'm mentally numb.
   Crazy, I just cannot bear.
   I'm living with something that just isn't fair.